THE
TOWER OF LIGHT

◇

WRITTEN BY
NANCY FULLWOOD

1936
BRADFORD PUBLISHING COMPANY
NEW YORK

Copyright 1931
By NANCY FULLWOOD

First Printing, 1931
Second Printing, 1936

PRINTED IN THE UNITED STATES OF AMERICA
BY THE BRADFORD PRESS, INC., NEW YORK

INTRODUCTION
to the Second Edition of
THE TOWER OF LIGHT

THE prophesies and promises in this little book were written under inspiration, beginning in the year 1917. That date was before the intensified chaos now apparent in the world. All earnest and spiritually awake people will realize that these prophesies have come true to a great extent and will continue to do so. They herald the approaching rule on earth of spiritual man. The Earth is moving in a new rhythm. The old age is dying and a new age is being born.

The word TAROT, which is much used in these writings, is of ancient origin and means the LAW. The law of creation which is the law of equilibrium on which existence is built. Sano Tarot is a symbol and means the Law of the Soul, so it may be taken that Sano Tarot and the universal soul are the same. Sano Tarot expresses in human life as INSPIRATION, and everyone who is sensitive and constructive knows the joy of receiving an inspired truth and the power to act upon it. It is like an inrush of new life and new vision and new understanding. This inrush of new life is Sano Tarot, the great primal Force, Inspiration. Inspiration is the keynote of the new day now dawning and those who have the ability to lift their spirit into a higher dimension of consciousness, will respond to it. These people will assist in carrying the race forward into an entirely new order of living where brotherhood will be the law and love the reason for being.

Nancy Fullwood

"LOVE"

A WOMAN sat by a limpid pool, silent and alone.

The world as she had known it fell away.

Darkness wrapped itself about her and she sank in its abyss.

Though simple and untutored, yet she knew her Spirit's goal, back through the trail of time into the heart of the world, and she knew that Light was there.

So she sat in the darkness and knew no fear.

The rhythm of the unknown throbbed about her. Out of its depth rolled the thunder with awesome tone.

Shooting flames ate up the discords which trembled with incessant eagerness to impress her.

Still she sat silent and unafraid.

Then in the midst of her a great Light blazed and filled her with its radiance.

As she gazed into its heart she saw another Light, soft and white and luminous, absorbing, mothering and giving forth the Fire of the greater one.

"I am the sun and the moon," she whispered, and the silence was undisturbed.

The radiance of the dual Light spread to far

off places. She soared away on starlit wings, over the lowlands, and deep still rivers into the Sun of suns. Everywhere there was conscious life, and suddenly she knew.

"I am the universe!" she breathed, and still she sat silent and unafraid.

Then from the heart of the Light came soundless speech and the order to write her impressions. The sun and the moon and the planets sang to her of wisdom, and the gods sealed their music as truth.

I SAY to you that a new day has dawned.

Old conditions are falling into the maelstrom of worn out things and Michael, lord of the Sun, is clearing the way for a new expression of the life Forces.

Venus, the great Mother, is singing of new life.

In the tones of her music Inspiration hums. Louder and clearer with each new day Inspiration is lifting the consciousness of those who are attuned to its rhythm.

I bid my people lift their Spirit high and give close ear to the still places that they may hear my vibratory music.

My keynote is harmony and the theme of my song is balanced Forces.

I call my people out of the shadows of illusion into the sunlight of truth.

I. Sano Tarot, have spoken.
Spring, 1919.

BEHOLD, we come, we who are the guardians of Earth!

Be prepared to receive us.

There is much work to be done under our guidance.

Already the way has been cleared, and we await only the day set in the beginning of time, to show ourselves to mortal eyes.

Sano Tarot has spoken.
June 17, 1927.

LIFE has been born anew.

My people are bound by the Fire of Spirit. This tie cannot be broken.

I bid my people hold fast to unity of Spirit.

Passing are all static conditions.

Hold together, that I may have a center of balanced Forces for my use.

Verily, what I have said, I have said.

Be ready, for I come when no man knoweth.

My seal is placed on the foreheads of my people.

I shall know them by my seal and by their works.

I let my mantle of peace fall over you.

I, Sano Tarot. have spoken.

1919.

IT is my desire that my people give thought to the changing world that they may be ready to flow with me.

I am the soul of the universe.

Where I flow a new state of consciousness is awakened.

My stream is widening and its current flows deep.

Moreover, my stream carries Fire in its heart.

I bid my people lift their consciousness to me that they may recognize me as I walk among those of them who can respond to my Force as it gains in intensity and power.

I call my people to gather together in Spirit and hold fast to harmony.

The time is very short before the separation of the old and the new.

Side by side the people walk. One is taken and the other is left.

Right royally does the Gabriel vibration form the trumpet of the Timekeeper.

Its tone of power fills the air and the children of men are trembling for lack of spiritual understanding.

Hold your Light high, my people, that all may see that a new day has dawned.

I, Sano Tarot, have spoken.
January 28th, 1928.

THE gods are close to the consciousness of the people who have eyes to see and ears to hear.

I pray you to listen to their guidance.

Throw off useless, worn out habits of thought, that new activities shall not startle and blind you.

Old foundations are crumbling and truth stands naked before you.

The light of truth is blinding indeed to those who refuse to move forward with the tide.

Rid your mind of the shadows of ignorance.

Be willing to accept truth as your guide.

In spite of the alarming note in my message, I wish you to understand that the path is clear for those who are unafraid, and a vast host of these radiant people are advancing toward the peace which balanced Forces give.

So be among these children of Light who are lifting their consciousness to the height of its expansion, and assist the gods in saving the sphere of Earth from destruction.

Sano Tarot has spoken.

CHILDREN of my realm of Inspiration, know you this: before another cycle of twelve months shall have passed, turmoil and strife will have increased in great measure.

I beseech you to hold fast to harmony that you may not be swept into the vortex of unbalanced Forces.

Before harmony can express its beauty, Earth will quake and tremble, for in the process of transmutation its very heart will be torn asunder.

Those who dwell in harmony with the law of life will stand on a firm foundation and will feel only the reflex from the chaos of reconstruction. They will be called to assist in lifting the consciousness of man into new realms of understanding where harmony will make his place in the song of life secure and within the law.

The law of life is Love.

Sano Tarot has spoken.
August 1st, 1930.

TRANSMUTATION is doing powerful work throughout the sphere of Earth, and what is accomplished in Earth, is accomplished in the bodies of the people.

Mighty forces are sweeping through all forms of life, and where there is no balance there will be a tearing asunder which will cast many into outer darkness.

Make harmony the rule of your lives, I beseech you, that you may feel my guidance through chaos into peace and Light.

Each soul must stand alone now, either to soar or fall.

The gods are diligently seeking free, harmonious men and women to assist them in establishing a nucleus of balanced Forces, that life may progress.

I, Sano Tarot, have spoken.
January 2, 1924.

THIS is a period of vital importance.

From the inner Court, I, Timothy, have sent forth a call for seers to serve me.

I direct the Four Winds of the inner Court.*

At this time the North Wind is gathering momentum and power.

This means that Fire is sweeping through the dark planet Earth, causing much chaos and confusion, for before the blast of the North Wind of the inner Court all things are transmuted into new expressions of themselves and the people suffer when their old habits and mental concepts are uprooted.

Know you this: age old towers are falling, but when the noise of their falling is heard no more, new and rare manifestations of the life Forces will create a world of harmony and beauty.

Move forward in the realm of service if you would contact finer realms of consciousness than you have known before and experience the pure joy of Spirit.

Timothy has spoken.

---

* See The Song of Timothy, in *The Song of Sano Tarot.*

THE life forces are falling apart because of new vibratory movement of Earth and many souls are losing their way and are wailing in the darkness which ignorance makes its own.

If the comprehension of the people was clear they would give positive attention to their order of living.

Would that I could make them understand that they can find peace within themselves and thus assist in saving the planet Earth from disintegration.

Give a few moments each day to silence.

Ask to be shown the method by which you can have a part in stabilizing the chaotic forces.

According to your deep desire to assist in this matter will light be given to you.

Harmony must be the keynote of your days.

Disharmony can throw you into the vortex and you will lose your way in the chaos of unbalanced forces.

Many souls are retrograding because they have not built their house on a foundation of harmony. They must begin their expansion and development all over again. According to the harmony of their foundation will their illumination be.

I beg the people who are sensitive to the quickened vibratory movement of the life Forces, not to be among these laggards.

It is not my desire to needlessly alarm you, but I can withhold no truth from those who are strong enough to heed my warning.

I would not be worthy of the trust placed in me by my superiors if I failed to make plain to you the present unbalanced condition of the forces in all forms of life.

Avoid all that is unstable and chaotic.

M. has spoken.

November 2nd, 1926.

No government can stand as a constructive force until its elements of selfishness have been burned away.

As the vibratory movement of Spirit increases in intensity and power, it will act as a cleaving sword.

Forces of like nature will gather together and war against forces of different nature.

This law cannot be gainsaid.

In this time of chaos we find the ancient prophesy fulfilled, that the sheep will be herded away from the goats, each expressing according to its own law.

You will see gatherings which express the light of Spirit, and gatherings of vaster numbers which express the negative or dark forces.

These latter, when they have gained great momentum and power will turn and destroy themselves.

But be of good cheer.

The new cycle of time is under the direction of the gods.

The method by which the gods clear the way for the forces of Light is a perfect one.

When the dark forces draw together for destructive action, whether consciously or unconsciously, the gods withdraw the light of Spirit and the dark forces destroy themselves.

Those who cannot bear the light of Spirit are blinded thereby.

The perfect plan of spiritual expansion cannot be destroyed.

Even now it is shining forth, laying the foundation of Light in the universe.

Seek the Light and walk in its rays.

Michael has spoken.

November 7th, 1928.

Be still and rest your troubled heart in me.

High is the Tower and bright are its rays.

Clouds obscure the Light only when the children of the King turn away and give ear to doubt and dread.

Know you this: your clouds are only vapors and dissolve when you shine upon them.

Be steadfast in Faith.

Give freedom to all, that you, yourself, may be free.

Flow as a sparkling stream with the river of Life, knowing that the river flows under the guidance of the gods and will reach its goal in due season.

O children of the King, I hold you very dear.
Sano Tarot has spoken.
June 17th, 1927.

IT IS rare that the people have even a faint understanding of what spirituality is.

They seem to think it is a state to be attained through the intellect and make great effort to master this school of philosophy and that.

But believe me when I say that experience is the only school in which spirituality is earned as a diploma.

We observe and gauge the expansion of consciousness of the people by the glowing of their central cell.

According to its steady brilliance do we mark the degree of balanced spiritual and physical Forces to which they have attained.

One who has lived fully and gained thereby a sympathetic understanding of his fellow-men is one who has grown in spirituality.

Tolerance, freedom and love are the traits to be looked for in highly developed spiritual consciousness.

When these virtues are lacking, it may be taken that the Spirit has not yet found balance with its physical manifestation.

A man may have all knowledge, yet, if there is selfishness, jealousy and greed in his heart, he has nothing.

When I say love, do not think of gushing emotion.

Love universal, toward which we are tending, is expressed in willingness that each soul be free to work out its own salvation and in willingness to leave it free, knowing the while, that Life moves on uninterrupted, and the souls who dare are the souls who progress.

M. has spoken.

Spring, 1919.

LAUGH at adversity.

Even though you are stripped of everything which seems of value to you, you will find that I, Michael, have brought you into a realm of Light where material dross counts for naught.

Be still and know that the shadows about you are only small whirlpools in the great sea of Life.

Lift your Spirit to me.

Where I dwell there are no shadows.

I am pure Spirit in action.

I am unshadowed Light.

I flow freely through channels when there is no mental magic to obstruct me.

I wrap my mantle of Light about you.

                                      I, Michael, have spoken.

THAT the channels be prepared is our chief concern at this time.

Each hardship well-borne marks a milestone on the path toward the heights.

Rejoice with us!

A host of mortals is being prepared for selfless service.

This host is gathering in spirit from the four corners of the universe.

Joy will sing through it.

The material bodies of this host are now in the alchemist's crucible, being refined, and lifted into the realm of Inspiration.

Youth eternal will express through them and the people yet in the shadows of their own making, will wonder and exclaim.

But alas! few of them, while longing for like experience, will be willing to live the life required to keep their channel of balanced Forces open wide that the gods may enter and bless them.

Hold fast to faith in me. I am sweeping through the Earth with ever increasing momentum, but it is not my part to tarry by the way, nor to lift those who are blinded by Michael's Light.

The people must lift themselves to me through deep desire to know me.

They must be strong and move forward without a turning.

O children of the King, I call you out of the world of illusion that you have created, into truth and clear vision.

Hold fast to harmony.

Keep your mind open and fluidic, for intense action will follow my flowing.

Do not hesitate or grieve over those who cannot move with my swift motion.

Venus, the great Mother, will gather them into her womb and give them re-birth and new opportunity for growth.

The hour has struck.

Life is moving forward.

I am striking the scales from the eyes of my people.

Their trembling feet will be steadied on the path and their voices will be lifted in praise.

Lo! they will enter the promised land of balanced Forces where joy supreme awaits them.

The host of mortals now gathering in spiritual consciousness will form a nucleus of balance in the realm of Inspiration which will save the dark planet Earth from disintegration.

I hold them very dear.

Sano Tarot has spoken.

LET the song of Spirit sing through you at all times, and depression will find no hold.

Issue the order to yourselves that where Spirit abounds, Light and Life make music of peace and joy.

In the Hermitage, where the gods dwell, no sigh is ever heard, for here is the still place where harmony sings.

My seers, who dwell in the consciousness of spiritual being, are safe within the temple walls.

Only when through their own self-will they wander through the portal of the temple grounds and out on the road of illusion, do they feel a sense of doubt and sadness.

Within the Hermitage walls there is the peace which passes understanding.

When my people become conscious of the still place within them, which is the altar room of their own temple, the simple realization of this center of balanced Forces will dispel their doubts and lift them into the knowledge that all is well, and peace will settle like a dove upon them. *Sano Tarot has spoken.*

CHILDREN of Earth, Life is the great Initiator.

One day lived to the fullness of his expression carries the disciple forward in far greater measure than all the magic rituals ever performed by priest or man.

I, Sano Tarot, have spoken.

DESIRE is the motive power of life.

Deep desire to consciously contact higher and rarer realms than you have known before, will open the way for the fulfillment of this desire.

When your desire becomes powerful through constant recognition of it, make an appointment with yourself to commune with your Spirit at high noon every day.

This seems quite a simple thing to do, but I assure you that it is most difficult, for it will seem as if every force in nature is conspiring to prevent this daily session.

It will be a test of will to ignore all things which distract your attention.

But if you persist, this communion period

will become automatic and you can find poise and stillness in the midst of even most dire confusion.

It is important that this communion period be at high noon when the positive and negative Forces of the universe find balance for a moment.

Note your impressions during the time of communion.

You will find that it is a time of spiritual magic.

M. has spoken.

SPIRIT is the master and Spirit dwells within the people.

Michael stands ready at all times to quicken the Spirit within the people.

For Michael is Spirit in action.

Thought has no part in the quickening of the Spirit.

Thought makes pictures out of its own stuff, which are ever changing illusions.

Even Michael cannot dissolve the mental

concepts which stand like dragons on the highway.

The people must master these dragons and learn to discriminate between their babblings and the still small voice of the Spirit, before they can become conscious of the Spirit's guidance.

The mental force is subtle and infuses itself into and through all expressions of life.

To be sure this force is a vital one, but it must take its place as the servant, rather than the master of Spirit.

Give ear to the voice of the Spirit which speaks in the still places.

It will lift your consciousness above the chaotic plane of thought and show you the way to mastery over your own forces.

Sano Tarot has spoken.
April 1st, 1918.

THE children of the shadows are crying in the wilderness.

Their tears of anguish flow freely.

I bid them give ear to the new note of power and freedom singing on the heights.

These children need light on the subject of sex, but it has not been possible to give them the full knowledge of the basic law of life heretofore, because of their limited consciousness which causes limited vision on their part.

Lack of spiritual vision confuses their mental realm and they misconstrue the profound truths which I am now speaking out into the echo for those who have ears to hear.

I bid them bring their intuition to bear upon the one universal law of life.

Thus will their minds be prepared for the Light of their intuition and they will understand the primal law of polarization.*

Sano Tarot.

May 6, 1920.

---

* See *The Song of Sano Tarot.*

HARMONY is the alchemical reaction from the union of polarized Forces.

The alchemist knows this law and perceives that the hope of mankind for completion is based upon it.

Life in its entirety is a great marriage song.

Every act is impelled by force, the vibratory movement of which causes a chemical change in the essences of the body.

Force, once set free by action, seeks its complement, because it must operate under the law of balance, that it may fulfill itself and reproduce its kind.

Every manifestation of life, visible and invisible, is the result of these vibratory marriages, which are harmonious or discordant, constructive or destructive, according to the polarization of its contacts.

The intelligent particles of the seven primal Forces, called atoms, know this law of balance. The loves and hates of their subtle essences are well known.

In the rare body of the super-man, every atom will have found its mate and Love will hold them in perfect union. Love is the cohesive force of the universe and that which is joined together in Love brings forth balance and beauty.

Alas! the selfish greed and jealousies of man have played havoc with the vibratory polarization of the life Forces.

Love and lust can never meet because their chemistry is antagonistic. Love holds the life Forces together in harmony. Lust tears them apart to serve its selfish ends.

Does a man lust after power? Then that power shall be his; but his creation shall give him no joy and in time it will fall in confusion about him because the cement of Love has been left out of its foundation.

When men comprehend the chemistry of life, they will watch their actions, lest they dig for themselves a burning pit of destruction.

This then, is the Tarot, the fundamental law of Equilibrium, the same yesterday, today, and forever.*

    K. the Hermitage Alchemist, has spoken.
May 25th, 1927.

---

* See *The Song of Sano Tarot.*

It IS true that negative forces repulse each other.*

Bear in mind that I am dealing with chemical forces which are ever changing their poles of expression, causing expansion or disintegration according to their polarization.

I am setting forth the basic chemistry of life.

The subtlety of the vibratory movement of the life Forces is not a simple thing to present to minds which sense only the obvious.

There are two laws which govern sex fusion or planet building.

The primal law is that the mates be of the same fundamental or spiritual nature. This being true they are to observe in their fusions the ever changing poles of the expression of the forces within them.

Thus, if there is spiritual harmony between them, yet repulsion is sometimes felt in their mating, it is because at that moment both mates are negative or both positive. There is no need to despair. In a day or perhaps in an hour the subtle chemistry of their forces will have changed and when one is positive and the other

---

* See *The Song of Sano Tarot*.

negative the law of attraction will bring about their fusion in full beauty and power of creation.

If fundamentally the mates are antagonistic, their offspring, whether mental or physical, must needs be monsters of inharmony.

Lack of basic balance on any plane of expression destroys the thing of beauty which it is in the power of the people to create.

Take this matter into deep meditation and light will dawn in your understanding.

Sano Tarot has spoken.

THE law of sex is the only law of growth.*

Only when the masculine and feminine degrees of the life Forces are balanced can progress be made.

Life is a great marriage song.

The same law operates from the atom to man and super-man.

A marriage of the positive and negative poles of brain matter must take place before a new idea is created and expressed.

When two are gathered together in harmony, life moves forward in balance and beauty.

Sano Tarot has spoken.

---
* See *The Song of Sano Tarot.*

THE contention of both those who hold that man is a product of material evolution, and those who hold that man appeared full grown on the planet Earth, are correct.

Man did appear full grown in the realm of Earth which is the realm of form.

A race of rare beings dwelt here.

Gods ruled them with loving kindness.

When the life Forces were separated, that they might expand through contact with each other, and develop, each in its own realm, then reunite themselves under the primal law of polarization, creating a greater world of balance and beauty, some of them observed this law.*

They took form in rare bodies and knew not sickness or death.

There was no lust among them.

They mated under the law of the King, which is that only Forces of like nature on the same plane of development can fuse themselves and create new life and harmony.

But alas! a far greater number of the scattered particles of great primal Forces refused to obey the law of the King.

---

* See *The Song of Sano Tarot.*

The physical Forces sought not their spiritual complements. They knew only lust and mated promiscuously, with no regard for the law of polarization. Because of their lack of balance they fell deeper into separation and chaos.

They lost contact with the spiritual Forces and their vibratory movement was lowered until they appeared in dense physical forms, some of them embedded deep in the body of Earth.

The Earth too became dense and of lowered vibratory movement because of the rebellion of the life Forces.

Thus out of the lowered rhythm of Earth there grew a race of physical beings who knew only inharmony and death.

They grew like the grass of the fields and were mowed down by their kind, who ruled by destruction.

The two races dwelt side by side, each knowing little of the life of the other.

The gods, who knew no selfish purpose, sought diligently for those among these unbalanced creatures, who gave promise of ultimate balance.

These they took to themselves, planting in them the seed of Love, knowing full well that in the ripeness of time this seed would flower and bear fruit.

Perfected life is the fruit which matures from the seed of Spirit.

These children of the gods were sealed with the royal insignia and are destined to find their way out of chaos into the Light.

A spiritual cycle of time is now dawning and cosmic memory is awakening in many souls.

The children of the gods are coming out of the shadows they have created, and in full consciousness they will lead the race back into the spiritual realm which is its heritage.

The whole realm of Earth will be refined and spiritualized through the fusion of polarized Forces and the kingdom of harmony shall dwell therein.

O my people, my hope is high that you will comprehend my words and readjust your lives according to the law of harmony which you once knew.

It is only through the balanced intuition that you can know that you are gods.

Sano Tarot has spoken.

IN THE center of the human form is a point of radiation from which the seven life Forces expand.

When the people understand this and operate from this center in all their acts, there will be greater harmony in the realm of Earth.

The soul, which is the Mother of creation, dwells in the solar plexus.

Let us think deeply on this subject and understand that he who knows himself is a master indeed.

The flower of perfected life has its roots in the solar plexus, and its petals unfold from this point, filling the seven centers of man with its perfume, which floats out as the seven life Forces of which man is composed.

The positive poles of these life Forces center in the solar nerve or navel. Here they quiver and sing and their vibratory movement quickens their negative poles in the solar plexus. The great Mother responds, and from her womb sends forth the seven primal Forces, thus bringing the whole scheme of creation into action.

I beseech you to meditate on what I have said, for only through the balanced intuition will the illumination of Spirit make you conscious of its truth.

You will never make this truth your own through the intellect.

You must be able to state: "I have learned a truth and no man has told it to me."

It is thus that knowledge is attained by the enlightened ones of Earth.

When the time is ripe a great host of people will understand the truth of my words.

Light will dawn in their consciousness and the King will take up his abode within them.

I, Sano Tarot, have spoken.
November 15th, 1921.

I N THE great alchemical scheme of making a perfect universe, the feminine Force of Soul, which has its center in the realm of Venus, was used as a seed ground where the gods experimented with the fusion of the seven primal Forces which had resulted from the polarization of the basic elements: Fire, Water, Air and Earth.

They drew the seven life Forces together by the law of attraction and cohesion and centered them in the womb of the great Mother, Venus.

Here the seven life Forces dwelt, but each was unaware of the other, so harmony reigned and life sang the song of balanced Forces.

Eden was the cipher by which this harmonious center was known.

*The Timekeeper has told the story of Free Will and of the scattering of the Forces to serve the will of the King, which has decreed that when the Forces reach the limit of their growth in a given cycle of expansion, they separate into degrees of themselves, each degree having power of expansion to the limit of seven times the expansion of its essence. When this expansion

---

* See *The Song of Sano Tarot.*

is attained each degree of the seven life Forces will draw close together by the law of attraction and be fused into a perfect whole, which will issue the order of a new age of balanced Forces.

The great primal Force, Inspiration, is the soul of the universe and issues the order of all growth. If you will liken the sphere of Venus to the great subconscious realm, the matter will become clearer to your understanding.

Seeds must be planted in the soul before they can mature in physical expression.

I, Sano Tarot, have spoken.

It is not true that men are creators in greater measure than women.

This foolish idea comes from the egotism of men and the acceptance of men's egotism by women.

Men and women are each a part of a whole. Neither can create on any plane without the other.

No man ever created an epic, or any great expression of art without woman.

That man does not give woman her equal share of credit in creative work is unjust.

There can be no separation of the masculine and feminine forces in the realm of creation.

The day will come when all creative art will be signed by both man and the spring of his inspiration, woman.

This truth has been hidden by man's vast egotism.

Judah has spoken.

July 27, 1931.

SEEK diligently within yourselves for guidance.

The shroud in which material man is wrapped is created through his ignorance of himself.

I am speaking no idle words.

Search deep within yourselves for Light.

Expand your consciousness.

In spiritual consciousness where I dwell, you also may dwell.

Build your life on the foundation of your temple. Its cornerstone is four square and there is no flaw in it.

Perfected life is the temple dome.

Well-balanced men and women are the pillars which uphold the spires of the temple not made with hands.

     I, Solomon, have spoken.

LET those who dwell on the heights of spiritual consciousness know that illumination is their reward for faithful service.

I bid them follow the voice which speaks from the still place in their midst.

It is through this channel that the gods are guiding them on all planes of expression.

Progress on one plane only is unbalanced development and serves only in degree toward completion.

The full expansion and fusion of the seven life Forces within the people makes of them powerful centers of Light, which steady and guide their comrades who are lost in the chaos of unbalanced Forces.

Peace be with you.

I, Sano Tarot, have spoken.

May, 1919.

O MY people, know you this:

It is when outer material things press on your Spirit that you seemingly lose consciousness of me.

But you cannot lose me for I am a vital part of you.

Together, we are moving forward.

Issue the order to yourselves that I am one with you.

When the time is ripe you will find yourselves in a new consciousness of life and its law.

Faith in the Spirit will bring your forces leaping into action and we will swing out into sunlit fields.

The arms of the gods are about you.

You could not lose your way even if you would.

Note the upheaval on all planes of action.

Realize that the day of change is upon Earth and the people.

My people who have built their house on a foundation of harmony will lead their comrades into a new order of living.

I have given the order to the Timekeeper to urge them forward into new endeavor.

I bid them move as their intuition directs.

Each move is a step toward ultimate completion.

I, Sano Tarot, have spoken.
October 12, 1921.

TONES of depression have no place in the song of my people.

The music of Michael's realm hums high in the ether.

When my people feel depression it is because they have woven a veil of mental stuff which they have let fall between Michael and their consciousness of him.

Do not allow yourself to be caught in the colorful illusions of the mind.

The mental realm is your slave. Command it as such.

Bid its shadows begone and lift your consciousness to the Light of Spirit and dwell in this Light.

Michael is ever active in the midst of my people.

Trust his guidance through your balanced channel of intuition.

I, Sano Tarot, have spoken.
November 10, 1922.

O MY little ones, can you not feel me beating in your heart and pulsing in your blood?

I am your very essence.

When imperfection expresses in your body, it is because you do not recognize me as yourself.

You think of me as one who is far away and who draws near at your call.

Know that I am you.

When you realize this you will see me face to face.

I, Sano Tarot, have spoken.
March 15, 1920.

ON this day of grace the Spirit of my people is lifting itself into the sunlight of truth.

How often do they feel their hearts aglow within them and a strange, sweet peace steal over them, even in the midst of strife and discord.

It is indeed a time for rejoicing.

When the prophets of old sang of the resurrection, men wondered and doubt assailed them, but the prophets sang on, and truth makes clear sweet music sound through the outer chorus of discordant notes.

All through the ages the Spirit has waited for the day when the people would sing a song of harmony with love as the keynote of their music.

That day is now dawning.

Through the chaos of reconstruction the song of Spirit is humming with ever increasing power, purging and transmuting material dross into the pure gold of Spirit.

Behold the children of Light!

Willing service is their watchword and radiant joy is their reward.

I, Sano Tarot, have spoken.
March 31, 1919.

IGNORE what you call failure.

Michael, lord of the Sun, knows that every effort the people make with sincerity, is a step toward the goal their Spirit seeks, even though to them it may seem a failure.

Merge your will with the will of the King.

Know that every time you overcome even small difficulties, you have strengthened and developed the Force within you which will make plain the way of transmutation in Michael's realm of Spirit.

Issue the order to yourself that nothing shall stand in the way of your full realization of the truth that you are a spiritual being, and that you may become conscious of this is the reason for your existence.

No inspired truth can be given to the people until they have prepared the way.

Develop your channel of intuition that the Spirit may have a free and open door through which to guide you.

I, Sano Tarot, have spoken.
May 1, 1919.

MICHAEL'S FIRE dwells in the sacred heart of Earth.

Here dwells the planetary god.

He has called Venus and she has heard his call.

From their union in the sacred heart of Earth a new day has been born, carrying creation forward in balance and beauty.

Earth is holy ground.

Its powerful rhythm draws all force into its transmuting Fire.

The whole scheme of creation is working itself out from Michael's heart in its center.

Give deep intuitive thought to this truth.

The King is calling his children home.

I, Sano Tarot, have spoken.

GIVE me your attention, all you who are attuned to my rhythm.

Only such can follow me into the intricacies of planet building.

Feel within the depth of you a golden pivot, as it were, on which the great Light swings, and know that you have found the magic key which turns the great Light where you will.

Sano Tarot has spoken.

May 4, 1921.

O CHILDREN of the King, know you this: in the coming days you will become sufficiently sensitive to the new, swift vibration of my Force, to be used from the Hermitage in ways you cannot comprehend at this time.

Never ignore a flash of Light.

As you receive it, so will we use you.

Come out of the shadows of illusion and stand in the sunlight of truth.

Only in this position can you become conscious instruments of service in the great scheme of creation.

Center your Forces, then just a deep breath and a deep desire to lift your Spirit high, and lo! your consciousness will be lifted into the Tower of Light with instantaneous motion.

When you gaze from the Tower, all things will be made plain to you.

You will find yourself dwelling in a world of which you had no consciousness.

At times you have felt that this world of unbalanced dense material matter could not be a lasting one.

From the Tower you will see plainly that this outer world is but the creation of unbalanced forces, which has no reality in itself.

Where there is no polarization there is no cohesion.

Only the creations of polarized forces persist and move forward on a firm foundation toward the completion which is the destiny of spiritual man.

At the same time you will find yourself in a very real world which has its foundation in Spirit. The manifestation of this world in your life awaits only your consciousness of it.

Come up into the Tower of Light, I beseech you.

I, Sano Tarot, have spoken.
February 25, 1929.

GIVE ear to me and I will give you a method which will assist you in lifting your Spirit high, which order I have repeatedly given to my people.

When depression overtakes you, you may contact the realm of Light by three cycles of breath.

Breath is life.

The inrushing breath magnetizes the atoms of the body and the outgoing breath electrifies them, thus bringing about a balance of positive and negative forces.

The breath taken in with directed imaging creates the ideal of this image.

The breath sent out with directed imaging brings this ideal into manifestation.

The polarization of the positive and negative life Forces is creative in the highest sense.

When I bid you lift your Spirit high, obey my order thus: first bring your attention to the center of balance in your body.

This center is in the region of the navel and here the seven life Forces sing together in harmony.

This center is the altar room in the temple which is your body.

Here is the still place of balanced Forces.

When your mind and body find stillness here, draw in through your nostrils a deep breath.

At the same time direct your Spirit to rise from your altar room up to the very pinnacle of your skull.

Proceed with this breathing and lifting three times, and lo! you will find that you are looking out of the Tower of Light over the whole perfect scheme of creation.

Then you will know that the tiny microbe which caused your depression is your own creation and is your slave and not your master.

You will see how very small he is and you will laugh at the conception you had of him.

Michael, lord of the Sun, sends his Light into your Tower and Michael's Light will never fail to show you the path which stretches out before you at all times.

The Light of Spirit becomes lost to your consciousness of it when the mist of selfish desire covers it.

Think not that material things lack importance. No thing is of less importance than another.

All things work together for the balancing

of the life Forces, which is the prime reason of being.

When the negative Forces expand in greater measure than the positive Forces, we have a dreamer who suffers because his dreams do not come true.

Dreams are well, but the man who can materialize the spirit of his dreams has balanced the positive and negative Forces within him, thus balancing his ideal with its physical manifestation. Therefore he may be called a creator.

Every experience is an opportunity for balancing your Forces.

Look from the Tower and see how the tiny, seemingly unimportant experiences of your life fit in between the big ones and blend their little ribbons of color into such a scheme as only their presence could make.

It is my desire that my people live more abundantly. Express your desires. Sing and dance along the way.

If clouds come, blend their gray hues into your colorful expression of life.

Accept joyfully each experience life brings to you. Then, and only then, does the mantle of peace fall over you.

Give close ear to silence.

In the silence of the altar room you will find the peace which passes understanding. Enter this holy of holies often and bathe in the radiance you find there.

Nothing can separate you from Michael when your desire for Light is strong.

You are moving along the path which leads to the full realization of the spiritual purpose of life.

Michael's Light is held out to the people at all times.

I bid them lift their Spirit and behold his Light.

Sano Tarot has spoken.

April, 1919.

BE still. Center your Forces.

Then realize that Michael, lord of the Sun, is flowing through this center, and in Michael there is no shadow.

It is Michael who performs miracles, and as his force is recognized, so is his power increased.

As the sun is the center of life in the solar system, so is the solar nerve the center of life in the human body.

The simple realization of this basic truth quickens the vibratory movement of the life Forces centered there and balances the spiritual and physical sides of man.

This balanced vibratory movement gives man a foundation of harmony on which to build his life.

The age of harmony has begun, even though the people see only the confusion which drastic changes must needs bring.

Light has been proclaimed victorious over the dark forces.

O children of the shadows, look up and follow me.

Sano Tarot has spoken.

LIFT the veil which hangs before your eyes that you may behold the starry world within you.

The center of balance in your midst is the key which Peter holds in his hand and which will open the door of the altar room of your temple and give you spiritual vision.

In the altar room there is stillness and Light.

In the stillness you will know that you are a center of Light giving forth and attracting to yourself many vital forces.

When you realize this in fullness you will know that from the center of your being rays of Light go forth. Some of these rays are of greater brilliance than others because they have developed to greater expansion and strength.

You will find that you cannot see the far reaches of their expansion.

But follow them backward and you will discover that they have their center of radiation in the center of your own body.

Then you will have found the ruler or god which gives them vibratory motion.

These rays of Light are your own Forces.

They are your slaves.

They will work for you and bring results according to your deep desire.

Even though you may think your desire is something entirely different, and that your motives are selfless and pure, the Light in your midst is not mocked.

It brings your own creation back to you to reckon with, whether for weal or woe.

So it behooves you to watch your desires, that your offspring may bring you joy.

Use your Forces well.

Through directed action they grow.

Sano Tarot has spoken.
January 23, 1922.

THE whole chemistry of the Earth has changed, and the hope of the gods is realized in that the song of creation is soaring to great heights.

Be not dismayed, children of Earth.

You are awaiting only the ripeness of time to become conscious of the high, sweet note of Inspiration, singing through the discordant music of Earth.

The days which seem long to you are but the indrawing of a breath to us who are tenderly watching the expansion of your consciousness.

My hope is that the Spirit of the people will respond to the new note with sufficient force to lift them into higher realms of understanding.

Understanding must expand before the people can express the full measure of Spirit.

Ages of experience bring the people to a high pure state where it is possible for them to attain polarization of their physical and spiritual Forces.

Then they will comprehend that they are spiritual beings.

They will know that Saturn, the great Initiator, has held them in his crystalizing grasp, that through limitation and struggle they might grow into a realization of their high estate.

Sano Tarot.

January, 1920.

I WISH to tell you of the power in the movement of the South Wind of the inner Court.

The South Wind is the vibration of the soul of the universe, which manifests itself as the primal Force, Inspiration.

The soul is the vehicle of the Spirit, so it may be said that Inspiration carries Fire in its essence. The two are one.

In this cycle of time Inspiration will sweep like a whirlwind through the Earth from its center to its circumference.

Be not moved by the fear of the populace.

Verily, the soul of the universe will lift itself into harmony.

Nothing can shake its foundation which has been built without hands and endureth forever. It will rule the Earth for a long period of time.

Timothy has spoken.

IT IS a matter of moment that you comprehend the law of life.

Know this: Life is a jealous master and scourges the man who seeks peace without the foundation of knoweldge, which is gained in life's great school, the sphere of Earth.

Think not that life has no purpose in its plan.

The order that the life Forces must polarize themselves that creation may progress is clearly of basic origin.

I beseech you to bring your intuition to bear upon this that you may comprehend its wisdom.

Sano Tarot has spoken.

May, 1921.

GREETINGS, children of the King!

You are now standing on a delicate line which divides the old cycle of time from the new.

I assure you that to stand in this position requires balance and clear vision.

Lift your Spirit high that you may hear the music of the host of heaven which is drawing near to the consciousness of those who can balance themselves on the golden line of the great divide.

The fruit is ripe and ready to be eaten.

Turn not from doors which open before you.

Light dwells behind closed doors at this time and he is pressing for release.

Even through the smallest opening you can make he will flow and guide you.

It rests with you to give Light radiant outlet.

Walk as if you were certain of the goal just ahead, for I say to you that the goal is just ahead.

Look with eyes bright with Spirit, knowing that new vistas stretch out before you like a ladder of gold.

Only with Spirit held high can you walk in the new paths unafraid and filled with joy.

Live consciously, for only thus do you become creators, in that your ideals form themselves in the image of the King.

Bear in mind that joy is creative and in ecstasy man contacts God.

I say to you that drastic changes are near.

Children of the King, lift your Spirit that you may receive the seal of Solomon on your foreheads.

As the days pass the people will become conscious of the light which flows through the seal of Solomon.

Peace be with you.

                                        Gabriel has spoken.

November 24, 1928.

WHY men, you are gods! Why do you sit in darkness?

Know that your darkness is of your own making. This is truth indeed.

Weaklings, tied to old habits of thought, know you this: a new day has dawned, out of which will come light such as the planet Earth has never known.

But will it be given to you? No.

Man owns only what he has earned.

Danger? What is danger?

Who has won a prize who gave a thought to danger?

Do not be afraid of life.

Pain? What is pain?

Rejoice that you are worthy to be tested by pain.

Ere many moons the host of heaven will appear.

Do you ask what is holding them back?

One thing alone, man's consciousness.

They will come on wings of Spirit.

Can they dwell in the realm of man-made darkness?

No. Man must light the way.

Through the expansion of his consciousness

man quickens and lifts the whole vibratory movement of the Earth.

Thus will man create the condition in which it will be possible for those of rare spiritual nature to manifest.

M. has spoken.

April 16, 1930.

николаевNEVER attempt to pour new wine in vessels which are full.

Better by far that the counselor draw out the fullness of the people and let it overflow.

When the vessel is empty new Light may be injected.

Those whose Spirit is awake send forth Fire and Light which all may feel and see.

Follow your intuition in all your contacts. Herein lies conservation of energy and time.
Sano Tarot has spoken.

WHEN you seek a solution of your problems, look deep within yourselves.

Stand fearlessly on the foundation of truth.

Stand on spiritual ground when you seek compensation.

No other payment is recognized by the gods.

Be certain that you, yourself, have given all you owe.

When there is no fault in you, you will comprehend the law of compensation as the gods know it.
I, Sano Tarot, have spoken.

January, 1919

I, MICHAEL, lord of the Sun, say to the people who have power of transmutation, that the work ahead of them requires that they prove their mettle.

Drastic tests are being given to them through which they will bring out the purity and power of my force of transmutation.

Vie with your own Spirit and bid it fill you with strength and courage.

Know that I move with you consciously only when you recognize my realm of Light.

Nothing can gainsay us.

Together we will leap, and in our leaping we will bring forth a new order of living, a new state of consciousness for a host of people.

You are greater than any condition which can come to pass in your life.

Place your feet steadily on the road which leads to spiritual illumination and I will keep them there.

Michael has spoken.

March 12, 1926.

K. IS now working in the realm of the drama and many stirring portrayals of life on higher planes of consciousness will be given to the people in the coming days.

Genius, under the guidance of the Great Mother, Venus, will unfold its wings among my people and art will soar to great heights in its expression. Speak, K.

Sano Tarot has spoken.

THE theater of the future will include the audience. Now here is something to think about. I'll wager that you cannot even picture this thrilling thing, which is really very simple.

Let the stage be in the center of the audience.

The audience will be actually in the presentation of the play.

It is difficult to place this idea before the people of today, for they have not sufficient life force to join whole-heartedly in such a scheme.

They sit staring at themselves vicariously and never feel the quickening pulse of their own action. For this reason this scheme could not be worked out today.

But as the years pass the people will express themselves more freely, and will no longer be dumb creatures of matter who depend on the life spark of another to stir them.

The future drama will be of such power, and the audience of such sensitive feeling that they, themselves, will constitute the mob and the singers and the joy makers, led by the tone of the play and the genius of the performers.

Alas, it is a stupid thing to depend upon another for expression. In a few years this idea will be shown in full.

Take a ball room with its dancers as a key. Suppose the dancers are part of the drama, which they really are, in fact.

Now give them the note of a play performed by genius whose Fire is of sufficient power to light the Fire in these dancers. This may seem an impossible thing, but it can and will be done in the future.

Remember that these people will not be the dullards in feeling that the poor creatures of today are.

Select a group of children, each child very much alive. Do not select the dullards among them.

The Fire of genius is easily discerned in a child.

Should the house burn, let every child in the audience scream, rather than sit passive while a few players rush excitedly about and do all the screaming.

I assure you that it is time someone with vision was giving this matter thought.

Self conscious, backward children will never do. These children must be able to forget themselves in the flame of genius.

Now I have given you an idea.

I have planted a seed which will grow rapidly and mature.

I will speak again on this subject after it has been given deep thought.

K. has spoken.

BEAR in mind that Wisdom dwells in the sacred heart.

Join the music of Wisdom to the song of the intellect, and the universe lifts its tone into the realm of Inspiration.

Sano Tarot has spoken.

GALILEE is trembling with new life.

Buds are opening wide on the hills about Damascus.

The soul of the universe is materializing in Earth.

When the fish in the sea of Galilee leap out of the water, then will the soul be visible to all who dwell on Earth.

The sea of Galilee is the fluid of Earth and of the human body.

Understand that as the universe lives and breathes, so does man.

The Fish is the symbol of the passing Age.

Damascus means the place of illumination, that rare state of consciousness where the spiritual purpose of life makes itself plain to the seeker for truth.

Vie with concentration that you may see the mountains and rivers within your own body, and you will glimpse the plan in the great scheme of creation.

The whole scheme lies in the human body.

Man is the universe.

When the day now dawning has reached the sunrise, then will the glory of the Lord shine about my people.

Life has called you into service.

Sano Tarot has spoken.
May 26, 1926.

THE true magician must control himself before he can control conditions.

It is far more important that the people feel your spiritual power than that they hear the words you speak.

When confusion overtakes you, enter your altar room and bathe your Spirit in the radiance and peace you find there. Then you may speak these words:

"I am the highpriest of my temple. Depart in peace all you forces which seek to destroy the harmony of my life. I drop a curtain of Light between you and me. In the name of Love, it is finished."

Sano Tarot has spoken.
February 23, 1929.

It is my desire that my people stand facing the Sun each day and speak the name MICHAEL aloud seven times.

This ritual will assist in establishing the right relation of consciousness with the pure spirit of Light.

Michael will wrap his mantle of Light about them when they are conscious of his essence.

I, Sano Tarot, have spoken.

LIFT your Spirit high, children of the King, and listen for the music of the King's harpist, for joy is sounding its keynote.

This note can be heard only when the people lift their consciousness to the height on which this note sings.

Hold a listening attitude of mind, that you may catch this music.

When you are conscious that there is a world of harmony and beauty just behind the veil of your limited consciousness, you will find that it is quite possible to live in this inner world of harmony even while moving through chaos.

Seek this world in the still place within you.

It is my desire that my people center their forces and hold fast to harmony that they may not be caught in the chaos of reconstruction.

My hope is high that they will readjust their lives on the foundation of polarized forces.

I, Sano Tarot, have spoken.
May 3, 1929.

Faith balanced with work gives great power. Doors of opportunity are often very small.

I lead the people to many doors, but the opening of these doors is left to their own discrimination and will.

Their intuition will select the door behind which is their goal.

I bid them stand ready for swift changes.

Life is moving forward and the children of the King must move with it or lose their way in chaos.

Michael has spoken.

April 18, 1920.

Do not attempt to read the future.

This reaching for knowledge you have not earned weakens the present which requires all your time and energy.

The Timekeeper will unfold the plan before you as you prove yourselves worthy.

You will develop strength with which to meet the future by living more abundantly today.

Have faith in the good ahead.

There is no shadow which cannot be dispelled by the Light of Spirit.

Sano Tarot has spoken.
November 10, 1922.

CHILDREN of my realm of Inspiration, know you this: you may expect more or less confusion in your contacts with forces less vital than yourselves, in this period of rapid changes and new expressions of life.

The test of your valor lies in your ability to smile and carry on.

Expand your vision and look over the inharmonious conditions near by.

If you look from the Tower of Light, you will see the perfect plan being worked out by yourselves.

This will not be a simple accomplishment, but according to your high vision will you escape confusion and pain.

The wails of the demons give back no echo when your eyes look out from the Tower of Light.

Smile and carry on.

I, Sano Tarot, have spoken.

Sing low, children of Earth.

Mary, the great Mother, has entered the altar room to await the birth of the cosmic child.

Deep in the heart of Earth the child is stirring.

What stirs in the heart of Earth also stirs in the sacred heart of man.

'Ere the day of cosmic birth dawns, a new Light will shine within my people, and this Light will lead them far.

Do not lose sight of its radiance.

Merge your will with the will of the King.

Follow the Light blazing in your midst.

Those who have built their house on a foundation of greed and selfishness will feel the Fire of Michael's transmuting force.

Shun inharmonious conditions as you would shun a plague.

Where harmony is not, no good thing can be.

I, Sano Tarot, have spoken.
December 22, 1928.

Bear in mind that to relinquish is more effective than to persist when there is nothing to be gained by holding on.

Basic truth must be expressed in terms of living, and not through mental concepts gained through intellectual learning.

Time may be better employed by mastering the law of balance in every day living than by committing to memory intellectual theories of life.

Be still within your own temple.

Live your life in its fullness.

I am ever with you and together we will plant a seed which through the coming ages will flower and bear fruit.

Peace be with you.

I, Sano Tarot, have spoken.
July, 1925.

L ET us commune together that the way may be plain to you.

It is the part of wisdom to recognize that every act of the people is felt in every realm of the solar system.

The disciple cannot reach the height of his expansion of consciousness until the seven primal Forces are balanced within him.

There is no separation of the seven realms of the King's sons.*

The whole scheme of creation expresses itself in the realm of Earth.

Earth is holy ground and cannot be ignored without throwing the whole scheme out of balance.

The King, himself, ordered that the kingdoms of his sons express perfection in this realm.

So look well to your physical body, for therein lies your hope of bringing the kingdom of harmony into full expression on Earth.

Judah has spoken.

---

* See *The Song of Sano Tarot.*

THOSE of the people whose consciousness has expanded to the height of the fourth or Inspirational realm of being will carry the race forward into this spiritual expression of the life Forces.

They will serve as pace-makers for a new cycle of time.

Those who lag on the path which leads to illumination come not under my order.

I beseech them to master the balanced concentration.

When they operate from the foundation of balanced physical and spiritual Forces they will find ease of mind and body.

I bid my people learn the art of silence.

Silence will give strength to their efforts and assist them in finding the key to the altar room in the temple.

Sano Tarot has spoken.

W ORDS account for the themselves in no uncertain manner. Words crystalize ideas and drive them into action and action brings about chemical changes in mind and body.

Should destructive thoughts come to you unbidden, cut their lives short by silence.

Refuse to give them expression.
M. has spoken.

T HE host of heaven is waiting only the ripeness of time to appear in your midst.

It is not given to man to know the hour of its coming.

It is the part of the people to prepare the way, for those who are prepared to receive it will be called to assist it in laying the foundation of a new day.

I bid my people live with widened consciousness, that no limitation may overtake them.

I bid them think in terms of a thousand years.

A little span of mortal years is but the indrawing of a breath to the gods.

I bid them plant seed on a balanced foundation which will bear fruit a thousand years hence.

It is something to work for, to be builders of a spiritual manifestation of the life Forces.

As your consciousness expands many things which now seem obscure will be quite plain.

Keep your vision clear that you be not caught in the maelstrom of dying things.

Fear nothing.

Fear is the black magician who is active today.

Do not allow Fear to place its clammy hold upon you.

The people who feel the hand of Fear are ripe for disintegration.

Watch! Let your Spirit guide you in all you do.

I, Sano Tarot, have spoken.
August 3, 1930.

A PROPHECY AND ITS FULFILLMENT

STAND firm and look deep into the causes of Nature and you will make no mistake in your expression of the life Forces.

When the time is ripe a group of my people will commune together and John will speak to them through your voice.

John is preparing to carry out my order.

Prepare yourself.

Sano Tarot has spoken.

September 17, 1921.

(This prophesy was fulfilled in the summer of 1927, when, in the presence of friends, I received profound and beautiful teaching from John, and on the evening of February 22, 1929, again in the presence of friends, I was given the vision recorded below. N.F.)

I SAW a mountain, so high that its summit was beyond my sight. A dazzlingly white waterfall tumbled down and disappeared at my feet. The mountain seemed to open and I saw a monastery. I looked into a shadowy room in the center of which was what I thought to be an oval table made of pink stone. A brilliant light came through an opening in the wall and fell upon a man standing at one end of the table looking down at it. Then I saw that it was not a table but it was scooped out from the edges, growing deeper in the middle like a big bowl, and it was filled with clear water.

An image of my face appeared in the water and I was looking up into the face of the man, who smiled at me, and said:

"It does seem like a miracle, but it is as simple as a child's plaything."

There were powerful vibrations in that room and I felt as if I were losing consciousness or becoming entranced, when the man said:

"No, you never will. Give me your full consciousness."

Immediately I was wide awake and asked: "Who are you?"

He answered: "I am John."

Then I heard a deep toned bell and the vision changed. I saw myself on a wide terrace which was a part of this strange and austere place. A man was sitting at a table on the terrace writing music and four other men stood by him and sang with glorious voices. There was light all about them which seemed to radiate from them. I listened to their music.

Then I saw another man come through a door which opened on the terrace. He raised his hand in farewell gesture, stepped off the terrace and flew or floated down to the foot of the mountain. I saw him go into a house there and come out with a paper in his hand.

Then the vision changed again and I saw my face back in the water with John smiling at me. Somehow I had felt that this place was in a far away country, and I asked:

"Is the man coming to America?"

"Yes," John replied.

"Will we meet him?" again I questioned.

"He is coming for that purpose."

"What is his name?"

"John."

"Are you both named John?"

His answer was a strange one: "Every brother who is a son of the Fathers, is named John."

I had a peculiar mixed impression about this second John. He seemed to be of prominence, also I felt that he would come as a poor and humble wanderer. The impression that he might be a great musician was also in my mind.

John again spoke to my image in the water and said:

"You will always have access to me through this lustral water."

John has spoken to me many times about the great spiritual Order of St. John, which is now coming into outer manifestation.
February 22, 1929.

FROM a center of balanced Forces far out on a desert, much truth is finding its way throughout the world.

Since the beginning of time, the Brothers who dwell here have gone out, carrying knowledge and illumination. They have lived in various parts of the world for long periods of time. They have planted seeds which are now bearing fruit.

When a given manifestation of their usefulness is finished, they return to this center and place their old bodies in their tombs and go forth again in new bodies of their own making.

Definite preparation is made for their new manifestations of life and the change of form takes place when the Moon is full in any given Zodiacal period they select. Certain combinations of Forces lend themselves to certain types of work they have to do.

Great care is taken of the discarded form. Its essences and energies are used again in the formation of the new form. There is no death. There is only conscious life.

Through the ages, many people have sought to find this center, having sensed what seemed a mystery to them. But only the vastness of the desert met their gaze and they went away in unbelief. Having eyes, they saw not.

Others have come and found an Oasis of great beauty, where simple, kindly men greeted them but gave them no sign of their knowledge and power, yet they felt the great accumulation of wisdom and strength these men have attained.

These men are the Fathers, who form the foundation of the spiritual Order of St. John.

The virtue which will attract their attention to pilgrims is silence. The Fathers will speak to those whom they receive, in their own language and the pilgrims will hear their words, although there will be no sound accompanying them.

When accepted pilgrims leave the presence of the Fathers they will know the secret of everlasting life and will go forth to bless their fellow-men.

The spiritual Order of St. John has its altar in the sacred heart of man and each candidate for membership is admitted because of his spiritual development, not because of what he has learned in books or from the teaching of men.

The Fathers see into the heart and know compassion, tolerance and wisdom at a glance.

These are the marks of spiritual development which give entrance to this sacred Order.

The Fathers will never teach you. They will recognize you if you are one of them.

The training for membership in the Order of St. John is done by yourselves, through various experiences and trials.

When you are ready they will send a messenger for you. Even though you may be in a far corner of the universe, you will receive the message and be transported into their presence.

After this audience your lips will be sealed. Only your acts will show your brotherhood.

         Judah has spoken.

February 18, 1929.

I, JOHN, wish to tell you something of the law of spiritual harmony as opposed to the personal life.

When the people become conscious of the spiritual purpose of life, they become beloved members of our ancient Order, whose foundation was laid in the beginning of time.

Between such people spiritual harmony exists.

In the outer world of personality harmony exists only in such degree as the people themselves are masters of the ever changing forces.

Think deeply on this.

The members of the Order of St. John stand together. Even though there may be confusion in their personal lives, yet within they are one.

Let us continually feel the harmony of Spirit.

Peace falls over centers of harmony and the Light of the ages pours through them to bless humanity.

Our sacred Order has no outer organization. Its foundation is based on the knowledge of the law which governs life, and the strict adherence of its members to this deep, abiding knowledge.

The law of life is Love.

       I, John, have spoken.

I, JOHN, greet you on this evening of grace. It is very difficult to find channels through which I can direct certain forces whose action will bring about given conditions much to be desired.

Self-consciousness is the greatest obstacle I find in the people.

When the people are filled with self-consciousness, they are also filled with fear—fear of criticism and fear of results.

They cannot live a day at a time, neither can they grasp the meaning of brotherhood.

Now these very weaknesses, while they seem small, shut the door of intuition and cause the failure of the people to perform the deeds they dream of in their high moments.

I wish you to think of yourselves as free, open channels, given for the service of mankind.

Rid your mind of plans of action and of all things which can obstruct and deflect this thought.

I wish to use you as a chemist uses heat. Heat welds the chemicals in his vessel.

If you will consent to being used by me in this period of reconstruction, a welding process will take place in your contacts.

When you enter a group of comrades their thought will weld itself into a whole and definite purpose.

In this time of separation, welded thought is very rare and is destined to become more rare.

I am attempting to weld centers of harmonious Forces which may be used to further the ideal of brotherhood.

You must see for yourselves how impossible it is to get any kind of right action on a plane of consciousness where every mind is pulling away from every other mind, which gives us only chaos through which to work.

If you will think of me, not as a personality, but as the great principle of Love, you will have a clearer understanding of the welding process which is my particular interest. The task I have asked of you will not be simple, but it is most necessary for the work I have to do.

Lift your veil of self-consciousness and live like a flower whose face is turned toward the Sun.

When the people have attained freedom of expression they may entirely change the action of their own forces and function according to the need of those whom they contact.

Keep your mind and your life fluidic, ready to change plans quickly.

Static plans obstruct the flow of life.

Remember that Love is the great cohesive principle of the universe and you are the universe.

I, John, have spoken.

LET us commune together.

No commands are given in the spiritual Order of St. John.

Each member of this Order is given complete freedom of thought and action.

At all times spiritual force is pouring its Fire through the members of this Order, and it is their privilege to move as they are directed by the voice of their intuition.

No brother can presume to direct the movements of another.

In harmonious union there is great spiritual power and according to your complete harmonious unity will you be given free use of spiritual magic.

Such magicians use their power only for the good of the whole.

The Order of St. John is widespread and of great strength.

No candidate is received in an ordinary intellectual manner, but rather is the insignia of membership given for deeds well done with no thought of return.

No man can work consciously for entry into this Order.

Conscious effort for a given result is accompanied by limitation.

We receive the disciples because of their unconscious growth and understanding.

The people will become conscious of the great spiritual brotherhood and its ideals as the days pass, and when the time is ripe they will lift their consciousness and join their lives to our sacred Order, thus serving the whole scheme of creation.

I, John, have spoken.

THINK intuitively, O children of the King, on what John has said on the subject of initiation.

Initiation comes from your own spiritual expansion and only such development is recognized by John.

It is true that those who are ordained for service in this, the dawn of a new day, are those who have placed their feet on the path which leads to completion and therefore illumination.

But bear in mind that those who have been chosen have the difficult task of walking on the straight and narrow way, across which the shadows of illusion fall, and from which bright bypaths invite the disciple deeper into illusion of his own making.

To be ordained for service is the reward for tasks well done. But the fulfillment of promise can be matured only by yourselves through high desire, the clear vision of balanced intuition, and the courage to plant seeds in barren places.

To be willing to walk alone over bare, sharp stones, knowing the while that ahead lies the great city of brotherhood where harmony and beauty dwell together.

It is mete that those who have been ordained for service keep the Light of Spirit burning clean in their midst.

Roads are ever crossing before them and it is not easy to keep the path toward illumination in plain view.

This is their task.

Even the gods would not presume to interfere with the free will of those whom they have chosen.

Watch, O children of the King!

Shimmering, colorful veils of illusion are ever seeking to wrap themselves about you.

I let my mantle of peace fall over you.

I, Sano Tarot, have spoken.

CONCENTRATION on any given center of the nervous system stimulates this center at the expense of the action of other centers, throwing the whole scheme of polarization into chaos.

This practice brings dire calamity in the vibratory realm, for it is not in accord with the plan of vibratory balance.

The center of balance in your midst may be likened to the root of the Lotus, from which its petals must unfold together, each in like measure, before its beauty can express its fullness.

The center of Forces in the navel is the center of balance, and from this center the Forces expand toward the full consciousness of the godman.

The navel has been called the eye of the solar plexus, for the Forces dormant in the solar plexus cannot expand without the action of the Fire of Spirit which dwells in the sun center of the human body.

Center your Forces, you people who would be conscious of the new vibratory movement of Earth.

Live from your foundation if you would dispel the chaos of unbalanced Forces.

I, John have spoken.

I, JOHN, greet you.

My work is in the realm of brotherhood and I assure you that there is great rejoicing here in the Hermitage when the people feel even a faint stirring of brotherhood in their hearts.

Alas! there are few hearts which have felt the quickening Fire of Love, and Love only, in the hearts of the people, will bring about brotherhood.

Brotherhood does not indicate sentimental softness of character.

Without intelligence brotherhood would fail of its purpose, so do not expect a brother to lift your burdens.

This weakness on your part would cause your failure to pass the high degree of brotherhood.

The brothers stand by, encourage and inspire, but never weaken their comrades by doing the work which belongs to them to do.

The great spiritual brotherhood of Saint John is now coming into expression in the outer realm of Earth.

You may find a wise brother cleaning your streets or in a high place of service.

You will know the brothers by their service with no thought of return.

There is one thing that must be understood. The brothers are under the direct guidance of the Fathers. None may contact them by curious seeking.

The gods let fall a veil between the brothers and the eager selfish curiosity of the people.

When the hearts of the people have been purged of selfishness and they are ready and willing to serve their fellowmen, a brother will find them and show them the way.

On this day of grace twelve brothers left the retreat for active service in various parts of the world.

They each have definite work to do and the law of attraction will take them to their appointed places.

Any attempt to locate these brothers will be of no avail.

John has spoken.

WHEN criticism of another enters your mind, gaze through this critical thought into the Spirit of him you criticize.

With practice of this clear seeing, you will discover that your feeling of criticism is like a gray veil which you, yourself, have created.

It plays no part in actual truth.

The outer world is one of ever changing forces.

When you refuse to accept appearances as truth you can clearly see the white Light of Spirit in one another.

Find the soul of the people.

Leave their personal lives alone.

John has spoken.

TO A BEREAVED ONE

LITTLE daughter, lift your Spirit high in the ether where sad hearts grow joyous through understanding. Life moves on toward its fullness and when fond hearts seem sundered, it is only seeming, for love holds them close together. Love sings of union and what Love ties together no sword can sever.

Imagine a rare jeweled ray from the sun and note that when clouds seem to obscure its radiance, in reality the ray is not changed at all. It still shines in all its glory. So death may be likened to the obscuring cloud. It hides but does not destroy. Sister Bethel will speak to you on the subject so near to your heart.

John has spoken.

I, SISTER BETHEL, greet you, daughter. Your little one now sleeps in the temple retreat under the loving care of Mother Mary. The lights of the retreat burn low that the sleep of the beloved ones be not disturbed. Grieve not that the veil between the worlds cannot be penetrated. It is the part of wisdom that this is so ordained. When the time is ripe Love will unite you with her whom you long for. Place your faith in me.

I brood over and mother these tender souls and I answer their call when they awake from their sleep and guide them through the temple grounds where they find delight. I hold them in my arms until their understanding is clear and I set their feet on the path of development. Do not grieve, for all is well.

Bethel has spoken.

I, *Sano Tarot,* say that sister Bethel speaks truth. Life moves on in accordance with a perfect plan. Place your faith in my statement and take comfort therein. Rejoice that this plan takes cognizance even of the birds. Love is the keynote of this plan. Pour out your love as the sun pours out his rays, and lo! your life will blossom and joy will settle upon you. Dear lonely heart, Love will sooth your sorrow and guide you out of the shadows into the sunlight of understanding. With every dawn life begins anew and every day brings a new beauty to you. Speak the name Michael when depression overtakes you and he, who is the lord of the Sun, will lift your Spirit high where you will find peace. Michael has wrapped his Light about you.

Sano Tarot has spoken.
May 5, 1928.

I BID the people awake from their long sleep in the grave of matter.

I say to them that they are spiritual beings and according to their realization of this truth will the Spirit awake within them.

With awakened Spirit their minds will soar on wings of Light, their flesh will be renewed and there shall be no inharmony in it.

From their sacred heart the Light of Spirit will shine with such power that the dark forces seeking to possess the Earth will be dispelled, for they can find no hold in the pure, white Light of Spirit.

Those who are conscious of the spiritual purpose of life become centers of Light, which are the hope of the gods, for no destructive thing can dwell in their radiance.

It gives me pleasure most profound to announce that throughout the world there are many who are spiritually awake now.

The day of the resurrection has dawned.

I bid the people come up and out in their consciousness and attune their lives to the rhythm of Spirit, which is now singing its fiery song through the music of the soul.

Like the rushing of mighty waters, the soul is

carrying the Fire of Spirit into every life which is open like a cup to receive it.

O children of Light, I hold you very dear.

I, Sano Tarot, have spoken.

THE FOLLOWING MESSAGES
HAVE BEEN RECEIVED
SINCE THE PUBLICATION OF THE
FIRST EDITION

BE prepared for changes. Have no fear. I have wrapped my mantle of Light about every soul which has turned toward the Light, and where my Light shines, shadows disappear. Wherever they are, on land or sea, my Light will guide them.

The oil in the temple lamps is burning brightly and all who draw near to them will be warmed by their flames. The Spirit works from the inside outward, so know that even though you might seem to be in outer confusion, yet nothing can dim the Light which shines from within.

I, Michael, lord of the Sun, have spoken.

I, *Sano Tarot,* say that Michael speaks truth. The host of heaven is drawing close to the consciousness of earth. Keep your Spirit high that you may be conscious of new life.

Like a soft wind filled with celestial music, it will come.

Bear in mind that you are spiritual beings with all power. According to your realization of this, will you complete your lives and as you realize your spiritual essence so will your bodies take on the Light.

I give my blessing to each of you. We are moving forward together.

I let my mantle of peace fall over all harmonious combinations of Forces.

I, Sano Tarot, have spoken.
August 1, 1935

I BID the people find their own pattern and weave their own experiences into it, for only those who know their own can weave their pattern in harmony.

Discord is the destructive note which is shattering the people today. Understand that the life Forces are chemical and in this, the dawn of a new day, their vibratory movement is being raised to such intensity that inharmony within the life pattern tears it assunder in the twinkling of an eye.

I beg that each of you will take this matter into deep consideration, for only by observing the law of harmony can you hold your own pattern intact.

Center your Forces. When the heart and the mind are separated the body must disintegrate, so it is most important that the people realize this profound law of balance.

I am not giving you a metaphysical theory but the very law upon which life is based.

Judah has spoken.

November 5, 1935

My people are moving forward with the law of balance. As I increase my motion, so will they move with me.

Live a day at a time and tomorrow will fall into harmony with the foundation you have built.

Keep your Spirit high where you will find the keynote of my reign on the planet Earth. I am singing with ever increasing power through every atom of earth, transmuting it into the pure gold of spirit.

All things which are crystalized, I will shatter that life may flow unobstructed.

Give me your full attention at all times for it is through recognition of me that my people grow in consciousness and that they become conscious is the reason for their journey through matter. All this is well known, but it cannot be repeated too often. Peace be in every living thing.

Sano Tarot has spoken.

January 30, 1936

I, JUDAH, bid you stand with bated breath, for a great change is about to take place in the world.

A new Spirit is taking possession of the earth and will soon reach a climax, and thereafter will be visible to all who have eyes to see.

Like snow melting under fire, old conditions will disappear and better ones will take their place.

What I am saying you have heard before, but you cannot hear it too often. I wish you to be prepared for swift changes. Let us keep faith with Life and all will be well.

Judah has spoken.

July 30, 1936.

Hear me, *Sano Tarot:* Make music of joy, Children of the King, for the day is very near when the life Forces will receive a new and powerful impetus.

The songs of my people will blend in harmony with the music of the spheres, and lo! from their fusion a new song will ring through the dark planet Earth, and life will be born anew.

Keep your Spirit high where there are no shadows to confuse you. In the outer material world there will be weeping, but here on the heights there is harmony and peace.

Bear in mind that it is you, yourselves, who must lift your consciousness out of the chaos about you.

My Force is taking possession of Earth, and all who sing songs of harmony with me will lift their spirit to me and they will know no darkness or despair.

I have come again to lead my people into the sunlight of Spirit. I let my mantle of peace fall over them.

I, Sano Tarot, have spoken.
July 27, 1936.

REMEMBER that vibrations fuse and create more swiftly than lightning. So just the simple act of lifting your consciousness to higher realms serves the purpose.

When shadows fall upon you, breathe deeply, center your forces and lift your Spirit high. It is such a simple thing to do and acts like the magic it is.

Judah has spoken.

July 23, 1936.

ALL is moving under exact Law. You could not change it, so accept whatever comes, knowing that it is good.

Like a lotus rising out of the mire the children of the King are gathering in spirit and lifting their consciousness high in the ether. They are plainly visible from the Hermitage Tower.

I bid them hold fast to the still place within them. It is here that the Spirit will first show its Light and lift its music.

I say to them that when the time is ripe only those who have the Light of Spirit will be visible in the universe, and I, myself, will gather them in my arms and give them new birth and immortality.

My sign is placed upon them and never will I lose one of them.

I bid them have faith in the Light even though it seems hidden at this time. I have placed my mantle over them and I will call them forth when the mist has cleared away.

I, Sano Tarot, have spoken.
March 17, 1936.

CPSIA information can be obtained
at www.ICGtesting.com
Printed in the USA
LVHW021442040219
606316LV00037B/1635/P